DANCING WITH THE DEVIL

and other True Tales of Northern Witchcraft

Jo Bath

Tyne Bridge Publishing

Newcastle Libraries & Information Service

Acknowledgements:

The author would like to thank all those who helped make this book possible: the Public Record Office, Kew, and Northumberland Record Office, Morpeth, for help with original sources; the AHRB for funding my original research, and Vanessa Histon and Anna Flowers of Tyne Bridge Publishing for guidance in the writing of books; Tony Liddell and John Newton for discussion of all things 'witchy'; Andy and Olga Holdsworth for moral support; and my parents for that first *Meg and Mog* book. Who knew where it would all end …

Dedicated to Holly, the newest of the Bath clan.

Illustrations are reproduced from the collections of Newcastle Libraries unless otherwise indicated. The majority of the woodcuts are from *Specimens of Early Wood Engraving*, William Dodd, 1862 and from *Bewick's Woodcuts*, 1870.

Tyne Bridge Publishing would like to thank Tony Liddell for the map on page 9 which he created from Speed's map of Northumberland, 1610. We would also like to thank Ann Caddel for help and advice.

©Jo Bath, 2002

ISBN: 1857951662

Published by
City of Newcastle upon Tyne
Education and Libraries Directorate
Newcastle Libraries & Information Service
Tyne Bridge Publishing, 2002

Front cover illustration: Women being hanged for witchcraft, from *England's Grievance Discovered in Relation to the Coal-Trade*, by Ralph Gardner, 1655.

Other books from Tyne Bridge Publishing which you may find interesting:
Ghosts of Grainger Town by Vanessa Histon.
Nightmare on Grey Street by Vanessa Histon (out of print, but available to borrow from your library).

Send for our catalogue:
Tyne Bridge Publishing
City Library
Princess Square
Newcastle upon Tyne
NE99 1DX

Find us on the web:
www.tynebridgepublishing.co.uk

INTRODUCTION

Whether or not we believe in magic, we all know – or think we know – what a witch looks like. Popular books and films are full of images of witchcraft, and a lot of them use the same stereotype – the old hag, pointed hat firmly on her head, stirring a cauldron, a broomstick or black cat by her side. But are they just stories to frighten naughty children, or did witches ever really exist? A few hundred years ago, most people would have told you quite firmly that yes, witches and magic were real, charms and curses worked. Hundreds of women were accused of witchcraft in court, and some were hanged for it. But people's ideas of what a witch looked like, how she acted, and how she could be stopped, were very different from ours. Here, using real testimonies from victims and eyewitnesses in the North-East, we will uncover the truth about witches, and why people were afraid of them.

CONTENTS

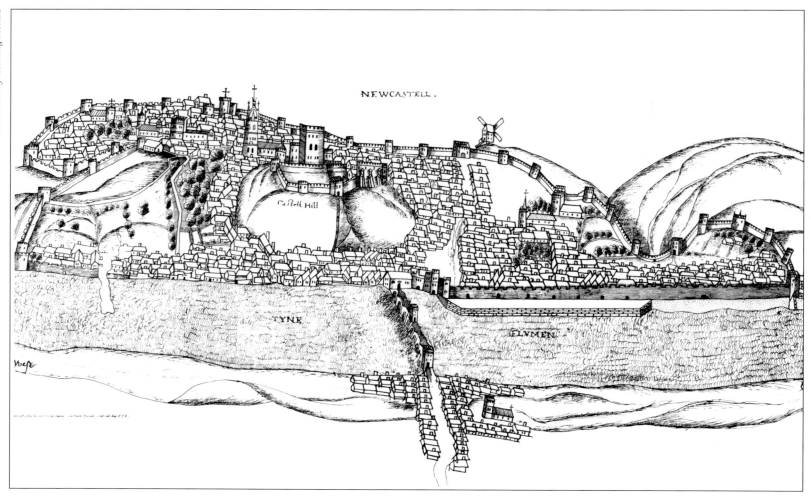

NEWCASTELL.

Castell Hill

TYNE

FLVMEN

West

This drawing from around 1590 is probably one of the earliest representations of Newcastle. It is still very recognisable, with the Castle Keep and St Nicholas's church just left of centre. Other landmarks, aside from the medieval Tyne Bridge, are St Andrew's church behind and to the left of St Nicholas's, St John's church further to the left of St Nicholas's, and the town wall.

CUNNING CRAFT

itches were around in the 13th century, and probably even earlier. But most stories of witchcraft and magic come from the 17th century, so that is the time we really need to understand. At that time, life was hard for many people in the North-East. Most people worked on the land, went to church on Sundays, and hoped that they and their families would escape disease, marry well, be able to pay their debts and keep their reputation in the eyes of their neighbours. Tyneside was a rapidly growing region of opportunity, but the new industrial workforce was poor and discontented, and Newcastle Corporation ruled with a rod of iron. The Civil War in the 1640s hit the region hard. Outbreaks of the plague made life even more unstable and uncertain. In the 1660s, forty per cent of households in Newcastle (including many of those mentioned below), did not have even a single fireplace.

A romanticised view of the old Tyne Bridge in Civil War times.

MEDIEVAL MAGIC AND WITCH MURDER

Belief in witches and magic goes back a long way in the North-East.

In 1279, John of Kerneslawe, Northumberland, was at prayer when a woman, believed to be a witch, entered his house. When he made the sign of the cross, she attacked him, and he had to defend himself 'as from a devil'. Without meaning to, he killed her. He was so shocked by his action that he became temporarily insane, or so he claimed. He ran away, but soon recovered his senses and took sanctuary with the Bishop. He was not tried, as he was not suspected of a serious crime, but he forfeit four pounds and five shillings of his goods. It's easy to assume that describing his victim as a witch was just to excuse his actions in killing her and then running from the scene of the crime, but others believed it too. By the agreement of all the clergy her body was burnt ... just in case.

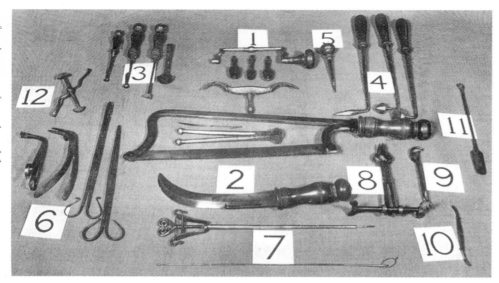

A set of Barber Surgeons' tools from the 18th century. No. 1 is a trepanning instrument for making a hole in the skull for relief of pain in the head – and to provide an exit for the disease, demon, or evil spirit. Operations were confined to the repair or amputation of limbs and external parts of the body. With no antiseptics mortality ran very high, so a magical cure might be seen as an attractive alternative.

Many people still believed in ghosts and fairies, even though the church said that they were impossible – a trick of the devil, or of the mind. And most people believed in witches, good and bad. It is to the good, or those who tried to do good, that we will look first.

Using the services of a 'cunning man' or 'cunning woman' – someone who claimed magical powers – was frowned on by authority, especially the church. But there were still quite a few people who offered to perform a variety of services for a small fee, or no fee at all. They specialised in solving problems which others could not help with.

For instance, many illnesses and injuries were beyond the skill of doctors. Only the richest could afford to be attended by highly trained physicians who combined medicines with other more exotic forms of treatment and diagnosis. Others turned to the barber-surgeon, who with a fearsome set of tools dealt with matters such as tooth extraction and amputation.

Apothecaries would sell herbal 'cures' for all manner of ills. But people did not understand diseases and their transmission, so cures were always hit and miss. And turning to someone who promised a magical cure made sense, as all medicine was mysterious.

Some women who built up a reputation for healing or other charms later found themselves feared and even accused of witchcraft. Even if they did nothing but perform healing magic or recite a few charms, this was still against church law. They were vulnerable to accusations by god-fearing locals or by vindictive clients when they were unsuccessful.

Punishments in these sorts of cases were usually designed to humiliate rather than hurt. Those found guilty would be forced to wear a white sheet and make a public confession of guilt in church. Sometimes the church also made the clients of a cunning person confess their sins publicly.

THE BREATH OF INNOCENTS

Mrs Pepper was a midwife in Newcastle, and highly respected. She was probably a Roman Catholic, and used bits and pieces of Roman ritual, combined with bits of much stranger charming, in her healing methods. Two testimonies from 1662 describe her methods. Her cures were unorthodox, even for the time, and seem to have raised suspicion that she was the cause of the problem in the first place.

Pit worker Robert Pyle was ill with head pains and a faint stomach, and his doctor seemed unable to help. He did suggest, though, that Robert send a sample of his urine to Mrs Pepper (urine was supposed to reveal a great deal about a person's state of health). Soon after he did this, Mrs Pepper arrived at Robert's house. She asked him to go to the door, and there something must have happened, as immediately afterwards he had to be dragged back in with one of his legs disabled. She gave him a bottle of 'water' – a spectator later claimed it was holy water – and sprinkled some on his face, calling it a medicine to be used sparingly when he took a fit.

She also laid a silver crucifix on a red hot spot on his right hand, and then his lips. Most strangely, she called for two small children, and put them near his mouth, since, she said, the breath of children would suck out the evil spirit which caused his troubles.

Not surprisingly, to the 21st century mind, none of this seems to have helped, and Robert became worse, and 'in a very sad and lamentable condition, to the astonishment … of all spectators'. Whether Mrs Pepper was blamed for causing the problem, failing to cure it, or just for her unusual methods (using innocent children to suck out evil spirits was surely asking for trouble), is unclear, but she was soon accused of witchcraft.

Even these practices were not as strange as those of Katherine Thompson and Anne Nevelson of Wooler. They were presented to the church court of Durham in 1604 as charmers, who 'bring white ducks or drakes, and to set the bill thereof to the mouth of the sick person'. At the same time they mumbled charms 'in such strange manner as is damnable and horrible'.

SINFUL MAGICS

The world was full of dangers and problems which could require the services of a charmer, especially if we look back to Tudor times. In 1570, Janet Pereson of Wallsend was accused of sinful magics because of her activities in healing those 'taken with the fairy'. She used the ancient practice of belt or girdle measuring – girdles were thought to alter sympathetically in size when someone was troubled by fairies. In one instance, she diagnosed a boy and prescribed the cure – two servants were to fetch some south running water, without speaking at all along the way. Then 'the child should be washed in that water, and dip the shirt in the water, and so hang upon a hedge all that night, and that on the morrow the shirt should be gone and the child should recover health'. They washed the shirt, and hung it up as requested (you have to wonder whether part of the scheme was an elaborate method of shirt theft!). But the shirt did not go, and presumably the child did not recover his health, as Janet was reported to the church courts soon afterwards.

HEALING AND HARMING

Trying to heal people, it seems, was inviting trouble. There was no clear distinction between those who had power to heal, and those who had power to harm, and the same person often built up a reputation for both things. Margaret Stothard of Edlingham in Northumberland was one such person, whose career of charming had spanned at least twelve years.

In 1671, Jane Carr was very worried about her child. A

strange woman had come up to it, and twice said 'here's a fine child' – and the child immediately began to cry and shriek. It doesn't seem to be a particularly unusual occurrence, but for some reason it worried Jane. She called in Margaret, already 'a reputed charmer for such distempers', who confirmed Jane's suspicions that the apparently harmless words had actually been a curse. Margaret whispered to the child, then (her method reminiscent of Mrs Pepper), she 'put her mouth to the child's mouth and made such a chirping and sucking that [Jane] thought that she had sucked the heart out of it'. Margaret said the child was now well enough, and went outside, sat on a stone, and 'began to rave herself, and rift and gaunt'. Then she went to a calf tied up in another room, presumably to pass the evil spirit that had possessed the child

into the animal. Then she left. Straight away, the calf went mad, and the Carrs were forced to kill it.

Others lost more than a calf from dealings with Margaret. In the same year, Alexander Nickle was living with his family in nearby Larbottle. Margaret asked them for alms, but Alexander's wife was afraid of her, having heard that she was a witch. She refused to help, or perhaps she simply had nothing to give. She thought no more of it, but one of her children told her that Margaret 'did wave at her mother a white thing three times'. The girl fell ill that night, saying that Margaret was 'pressing of me and like to break my back', and the next morning she died.

Despite this, Margaret continued to practise charming.

In 1678, Isabel Maine was working as a maid for Jacob Pearson of Titlington. She was in charge of the milk production. She suspected that a witch was at work as the milk was not curdling into cheese, so she asked a neighbour to consult Margaret Stothard. Butter and cheese-making was an important part of the household economy, so it was an enormous problem if anything happened to interfere with production. Margaret said she would sort out the problem. Eight days later she arrived at Titlington to confirm her success, and told

Edlingham Church with Edlingham Castle beyond, c.1900. Margaret Stothard seems to have been active in a number of villages around Edlingham in Northumberland in the 1670s.

SCOTLAND

Adapted from John Speed's map of Northumberland, 1610

Berwick

Holy Island

Site of witch activity

Wooler Chatton

Titlington

Edlingham
Larbottle

Brinkburn

Longwitton Ellington

Morpeth

NORTHUMBERLAND

Corbridge
Blackhall Newcastle Tynemouth
Riding Mill Wallsend

Isabel that 'ill eyes' had looked at the milk. She gave Isabel a piece of rowan tree wood to carry with her when she went milking, but Isabel put it to one side, 'thinking there was no need for any such thing' now that the cheese was fine. Rowan wood was supposed to be lucky, to keep out evil spirits. Margaret also gave Isabel instructions on how to stop the cows sweating so much as she milked them – she was to 'take salt and water and rub it upon their back', and also to put a little salt in the milking pail. Margaret refused to accept money as payment for this advice. Instead she asked for 'a little of anything', so Isabel gave her a fleece.

This was one example of Margaret using her powers for good. But at about the same time, John Mills, agent to the Swinburnes of Edlingham Castle, was lying in bed, unable to sleep when a great blast of wind gusted into the room. Something pressed 'a great weight upon his heart', giving a 'great cry like a cat'. Then he saw Margaret Stothard standing at his bed head. He called out 'witch', but then entered into a fit so violent that it woke his family – they 'were forced to hold him and could not get him holden'. This happened

several times, although reading the Bible sometimes lessened the fit. And in summer 1682, John was in town to pay his rent when he happened to pass by Margaret's door. Here he saw a 'flash of fire', but still made his way towards the door. Then his horse 'took a stand and would go neither back nor forward' until John had called upon the Lord for deliverance. He made his way home, so afraid that he called for other people to stay with him through the night in case she came to him again.

People definitely believed a woman like Margaret was equally capable of good and harm. But even those whose charms were apparently harmless could attract negative attention, not least the suspicion of fraud.

THE DOUBLE-CROSSING DETECTIVE

Many cunning men said they could find stolen goods. In the 17th century there was no police force. A few 'constables' tried to keep the peace, but the job of identifying and accusing suspects was almost entirely down to the victim. So any method which promised to name the guilty was worth trying.

In 1690, Newcastle yeoman William Landstaffe, was unlucky enough to have stolen from him £3 8s 6d – a sizeable sum of money in a time when many people only earned a few pennies each week. He was told that Edward Blackett could help him, as he could by magic 'discover where and how lost and stolen goods might be gotten again'. Edward was, or pretended to be, dumb, so when William explained his problem, Edward wrote down his terms – he said that he could bring back the stolen money, for a payment of fifteen shillings.

That is all we know, except that Edward was accused before magistrates. Perhaps William paid the fee, only to lose both it and the stolen cash …

These very old houses in the Cloth Market, Newcastle, photographed around 1858, give us some idea of what the town looked like in the late 17th century – small houses with steeply pitched roofs flanking narrow streets.

A NEW LEASE OF LIFE

Edward Blackett was not the first man to practise charms in Newcastle. Twenty years earlier, Peter Banks managed to get himself quite a reputation for magic before someone accused him of witchcraft, or possibly fraud. Again, the accusations show the range of different charms a cunning man might claim to be able to perform.

Banks' main source of income was the sale of 'leases … for term of years and life'. Customers paid him 20 shillings in exchange for a lease of one year during which, they believed, they would not die. This was popular amongst sailors in particular, who returned to continue the lease year after year. The lease was in the form of a paper on which was written the following charm:

> 'I charge you and all of you in the high sword name to assist and bless [the person] belonging to such and such a ship … from all rocks and sands, storms and tempests, thereunto belonging for this year'.

Not everyone thought that buying one of these leases was

money well spent. One woman found out that her husband, a shipwright, was paying Peter Banks, and in her anger burnt the paper. Banks told her that for this action she would never be worth a groat – a fourpenny piece, literally, though usually used to mean a small sum, especially as the groat had stopped being legal tender a few years before the conversation. It seems that he was right, as the fortunes of her family declined from that day.

Banks guaranteed longer life by the commanding of evil spirits (this was what made possible a criminal charge of witchcraft). He was also able to conjure spirits out of the sick. One Gateshead woman went to him for advice, and was diagnosed as being troubled by a spirit. For a fee, he wrote something on a piece of paper, which he said would conjure the spirit out of her once it was opened up. It seemed to work, and he was said to have done such work before, 'burning pieces of paper in the fire writ for that purpose, at times determined by numerology'.

One woman, in disagreement with Banks, had visions of him standing amongst flames. She wanted to make peace, to stop these visions, but Banks claimed that she was bewitched by someone else. He persuaded her to give him some of her hair, which he sealed in paper and returned to her to burn. This solved the problem.

MATRIMONIAL MAGIC

Peter Banks had one other claim. He could 'make people that had ill husbands be good to their wives', again by selling one year leases. This proved highly popular! In the 17th century there was no divorce, and only limited opportunity for separation following cruelty or adultery, so it's not surprising that a charm which guaranteed a kind and caring husband was much in demand. One woman paid ten shillings and two new shirts for a new lease of a year, after which time she did not renew. At this point her husband reverted to his old behaviour, becoming 'ill and untoward', rather than loving.

Nonetheless, with all the abilities Banks claimed to have – up to and including the ability to use magic to extend or shorten the span of a man's life by a year – it was not surprising he made enemies. Eventually he was taken to court for 'arts magic called charms and spells, and assuming upon

himself by the same art to procure safety at sea'. Still, he was then acquitted.

Magic might also be a tool in the battle of the sexes. In 1435 Margaret Lindsay of Edlingham, Northumberland, was insulted by three men who said that she and another woman 'planted a stake which tied up men's organs', making them impotent through magic. She said that this was slander, and successfully brought witnesses to demonstrate her good character. In 1444, two Durham women were presented as witches for telling single women how they could get the husbands they desired.

RIDDLE AND SHEARS

The reasons why such behaviour was frowned upon by church and state courts are explained in a 'confession', which Alice Swan was forced to make while standing in St Nicholas's Church, Newcastle, just after the Sunday sermon. She was guilty of 'turning the riddle and shears', a crime which requires some explanation.

Based on the same principle as a pendulum, it was the most common magical method of detecting a thief, and was also used to determine pregnancy. A pair of shears was set within the rim of 'a sieve or riddle', and two people each put the tops of both their forefingers on the top of the shears, allowing the sieve to move like a pendulum. The cunning person would then recite a charm similar to this:

St Nicholas's church from a drawing made by Buck in 1745. Alice Swan was made to confess her crime here.

'By St Peter and St Paul,
If [the suspect] has stolen [the victim's possession]
Turn about, riddle, shears and all.'

They repeated this charm, using the name of each suspect in turn, and when the right name was said, the sieve would turn. Using two people was supposed to prevent cheating, but the method might have worked to reveal subconscious suspicions. Also, such methods were sometimes used in the presence of suspects, so the true criminal might, through fear of discovery, give himself away.

Alice's punishment for this crime was typical. Probably wearing a white sheet, she was made to say that although such divination might seem a 'trifling matter', it was 'expressly forbidden by God's laws and the Queen's majesty, and cannot be done without a defection and mistrust to God, and some confidence to the devil'. She begged the forgiveness of those present and asked them to pray with her.

This kind of punishment was double edged. Some seem to have been shamed into better behaviour in future, but a few are known to have seen the public exposure as little more than an advertisement of their services!

Another method of telling fortunes was noted in 1451 when Alice Davison was accused of divination and medicine with 'lead, comb and iron'.

THE CLERICAL TIPSTER

The riddle and shears was not the only way of hunting for lost goods. A more learned man might use astrology and numerology, and consult almanacs, books which detailed events in the heavens and their implications for men. John Vaux, clerk of St Helens, Auckland, County Durham, in the 1630s, was also an astrologer who wrote his own almanac. Risking the wrath of his employers, the church, he consulted this guide and others at the communion table, and would give

THE

ROYAL
Fortune-Teller;

WITH THE

SIGNS of the TIMES,

AND

SCRIPTURE PROPHECIES.

Printed by J. Marshall,

IN THE OLD FLESH-MARKET, NEWCASTLE;

*Where may also be had, a large and curious Collection
of Songs, Ballads, Tales, Histories, &c*

Also School and Children's Books, Stationary, &c.

*Not John Vaux's almanac, but a later example, this locally printed pamphlet
dates from the 19th century.*

advice on a wide range of matters, including racing tips! He charged a shilling for finding a stolen mare, four shillings in coin and eight pence in drink for finding a horse and mare. He said these charges were just as 'was due to any lawyer for his fee' and justified astrology as coming from God. Not willing to pass up a business opportunity, he also used his communion table 'stall' to sell copies of his own book!

MAGIC AND THE CHURCH

This behaviour in a church was obviously frowned upon. But the church itself, whilst not promising to perform miracles, did, in the later middle ages, lay claim to certain abilities to bless and to ward off evil. For instance, in 1426 the accounts of the Bishop Durham have an interesting entry – payment made to the church for the signing of the cross with St Wilfrid's signet, on sixteen cattle, to ward off ill health. This was acceptable because the 'magical' power involved came straight from God via the established church. All other kinds of magic, to an orthodox Christian, must be the work of the devil and his minions. After the Reformation in the early 16th century, clerics were much less willing to use the 'magic' of the church. They were particularly keen to discredit the idea that God's power could pass into objects like saints' relics or holy water, which had the potential to allow the power to be harnessed by either clerics or ordinary people. This is why Mrs Pepper, with her holy water and crucifix, got into trouble, and why holy objects like blessed communion wafers were kept locked and safe.

A Mummified cat

With all these different supernatural influences at work – from angels and saints to devils and witches, fairies and ghosts – it is no wonder that many people tried to take matters into their hands by using home-made charms – which they might have thought of simply as recipes with words for added effect – and by following superstitions.

One striking, and rather macabre, example of this sort of attempt to keep good luck has survived to be photographed. In the middle of the 17th century, builders were working on a smart house on Pilgrim Street, a fashionable district in the centre of Newcastle. It was to be the home of Thomas Winship, a member of the Tanner's Guild, and a wealthy property owner. It's not the sort of place where we would expect to see the hand of superstition at work; but when the building was restored in the 1990s, archaeologists found the mummified remains of a cat, placed under the hearthstone. In fact, putting animals and even people under the walls or doorway of buildings in order to safeguard them from evil spirits dates back to prehistoric times, and cats were

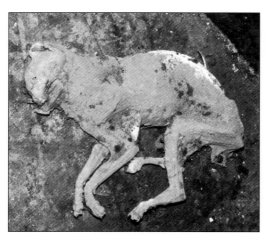

occasionally sealed into foundations as late as the 19th century. A few even have mummified mice along with them, and perhaps the cat spirit was thought to chase away vermin as well as evil!

Thomas Winship's home, now known as Alderman Fenwick's House, on Pilgrim Street, Newcastle, from a map of 1723. The house has recently been restored … but we don't know what happened to the remains of the unfortunate cat, so will its good luck continue?

The interior of Bessie Surtees House on Sandhill in 1933, showing us how a room in a well-to-do house might have looked in the late 17th century (bar the electric light!).

THE TRUTH ABOUT WITCHES

Most people think they know about witches – and it's all bad. Witches are gnarled old women who wear black clothes and pointed hats and ride on broomsticks to meetings of their coven. And of course, they always have a black cat. But there are a lot of differences between this fictional image of a witch and the way older accounts described them.

Witches were poor old women

This is actually true in the majority of English cases. There are plenty of exceptions, but when people thought of a witch, this is usually what came to mind. One book on the subject, from 1654, said that 'every old woman with a wrinkled face, a furred brow, a hairy lip, a gobber tooth … a skull cap on her head … a dog or cat by her side, is not only suspected but pronounced a witch'.

Witches wore black

Black is very rarely mentioned in descriptions of witches. In fact, most witches are actually described as wearing green, sometimes with brown or red. Green was a colour associated with the fairies and the supernatural, so if someone suspected of witchcraft wore green, it would strengthen the association in people's minds. Red was the other supernatural colour, and it was considered unlucky to wear green and red together, as this attracted the attentions of the fairies.

Witches wore pointed hats

In the 1640s, the common hat worn by women was black, and, if not pointed then at least tall and tapering. In the 1660s, there were many witch accusations. Most of those accused were poor and old, and probably the only people still wearing hats which were twenty years out of fashion.

Witches flew on broomsticks

Certainly some people thought witches could fly, but ideas about their vehicles varied. In the whole of England, there is only one accusation which mentions broomsticks, and this is from Somerset. In the north, witches seem to have just appeared where they wanted to be. In some instances, they flew by placing their feet on wooden platters which had never been wet. Anne Armstrong said that they used people as horses, as we will see on page 32.

as we will see on page 32.

Witches kept black cats

Witches were certainly thought to keep familiars, creatures which took on the shape of animals but were actually imps. They were not always cats, though – other possibilities included mice and toads – and the only direct mention locally is of a black greyhound.

Witches turned into black cats

Some accounts say that witches could turn into animals. In Anne Armstrong's story the witches take several forms. Dorothy Stranger (as we see on page 25) turned into a cat, but it was grey.

as we see on page 25

Witches met in covens of thirteen

The English witch seems, for the most part, to have been a solitary creature, perhaps acting with one or two friends. Anne Armstrong talked about covens of thirteen witches, so the idea was around, but it was more prevalent in Scotland and continental Europe.

Witches stuck pins into dolls

A few English witch accusations, including one of the earliest, from Saxon times describe this practice. But none of the North-Eastern witches used this method, as far as we know.

Witches brewed up potions in cauldrons

Every household had a cauldron – stew was a staple food. Shakespeare's witches in Macbeth used a cauldron and even then it was the stuff of legends. Witches by repute didn't need to use potions, but some cunning women might have brewed healing herbs this way.

WITCHES ON TRIAL

Acts of witchcraft contravened church law, which was binding on all Englishmen and women, but they were also in breach of secular law, so perpetrators could be tried by criminal courts. Exactly which acts were unlawful, and what punishment they warranted, varied over the years, but revolved around the conjuring of evil spirits, and acts of 'maleficia', magical damage. This usually meant causing illness or death in a victim using magical means. Those accused would be examined before a magistrate, a local gentleman who volunteered for the task out of a sense of duty or to raise his standing amongst his peers. If he thought there was a case to answer, the suspected witch was imprisoned until the next hearing of the assizes court – which in the North-East could mean up to a year. If found guilty, the punishment was hanging (not, as is commonly thought, burning). If the woman was pregnant the execution was postponed until after the birth, to avoid taking the innocent life of the child, and in practice this often meant that the extra time could be used to get a pardon.

Many accusations and examinations of suspects survive, and it is these which provide the tales below.

BEGGAR WOMEN

A pattern emerges in many seventeenth century accusations of witchcraft. Many of the accused were poor women, and relied on the support of their neighbours, to give alms, to lend items or buy produce. If help was refused bad feeling arose. Subsequently, if something bad happened to that neighbour or their property, it was all too easy to blame the beggar woman. This was especially likely where the woman

already had a reputation for witchcraft, a power which was thought to grow stronger with age. Some women must, over the years, have come to believe themselves witches, able to curse their neighbour successfully. It must have been very tempting for a poor, vulnerable woman, to play up to her reputation as a witch to gain some respect and frighten those who might do her harm. However, she was taking a big risk, and opinion could swiftly turn against her when someone fell ill, especially if the disease involved fits or weakness.

Sick people might believe themselves victims of witchcraft, or a doctor, faced with a disease he did not understand and could not cure, might diagnose unnatural influence. In either event, something had to be done. A common response was to try to 'draw blood' from the witch, preferably from the forehead, as this was thought to give relief to the sufferer. It also, therefore, proved suspicions about who was responsible. If drawing blood from a person helped the

CURSES AND BEWITCHINGS

Generally witches did not need complex methods to set evil spells in motion. In rare cases they might use a ritual form, as cunning men did in their attempts to relieve their bewitched clients, but usually their spell was simply words spoken in the hearing of the victim which carried with them a focussed desire to do harm. Such ill-wishing was listened to by the devil, and a successful curse was often the start of a suspicion of witchcraft, as the devil listened to his favourites most of all.

victim, them that person must have set the enchantment in the first place. This practice was well known and used often. Some argued that it worked because it cancelled out the effect of spells created by blood willingly given to familiar spirits or imps. But most people were probably just content to have something particular to do when faced with baffling and painful symptoms.

Prosecution and imprisonment of the witch was also thought to help relieve the symptoms, and of course a hanging, if it could be arranged, would bring complete relief (although hanging was generally reserved for suspects who were proved to have bewitched their victim to death).

BEWITCHED FOR A BEER

In 1660, fisherman's wife, Elizabeth Simpson, went to the house of Michael Mason, a Tynemouth soldier, and asked for a pot of small beer (this was a weak drink which was often preferred to water, as it was usually cleaner!). Michael's daughter Frances refused, and Elizabeth said she would make Frances repent the refusal. The next day, Frances lost the use of one leg, and was soon forced to her bed, where she said that 'Elizabeth Simpson did pinch her heart and pull her in pieces'. Michael brought Elizabeth to the house, and helped Francis to draw her blood, and this seemed to stop the pain although she continued to waste away. Michael also said that Elizabeth was well known to be a witch, and 'turns the sieve for money'.

THE WITCH UNDER THE BED

In 1661, the two children of Katherine Cudworth, wife of a Newcastle woollen draper, fell ill, and said that Jane Watson and Anne Mennin tormented them at night. Katherine knew Jane Watson well. She had been in the habit of buying a few oat cakes from her every week. But in the very week the children fell ill, she had been told about Jane's reputation – Jane was a 'medicer', a healer, with dubious methods. As early as 1653 she cured one Newcastle woman simply by speaking to her, and it was thought that the illness had gone into the family dog, who died later that week. When Katherine found out about this, she was determined to have nothing more to do with such a person, and sent her away. If Katherine hoped this would protect her and her family from Jane's supernatural powers, she was sorely mistaken.

One afternoon, the children, were in the house of Thomas Sherburn, a well-off watchmaker. They began to have fits, and servants and visitors crowded around to see what would happen. One of the children cried out that she could see Jane, and that Jane had brought her an apple, which she had left by the bed. By this point – probably amid mass hysteria – one of

Thomas Sherburn's house had six hearths, according to the Hearth Tax records, in an area averaging two. He lived in Heber Tower ward – around Pudding Chare and the Bigg Market, to the left side of this detail from 1745.

the servants also thought she could see the witch, a woman in a red waistcoat and green petticoat, who then apparently disappeared under the bed. One of those present, a Widdrington gentleman, responded in a most practical way – he thrust his rapier under the bed, and some there then heard a noise 'like a swine'. Then there was a 'flash of fire', and they saw 'a round thing like fire go towards the chimney', causing much alarm. Half an apple was found at the bed head, and the children got no better.

Jane was tried and found not guilty. Her fellow accused, Anne Mennin, was out of luck.

A witch for a wife

Anne Mennin was well known as a witch. Her husband of thirty years had thrown her out of the house and she was reduced to begging on the streets. Now she was imprisoned pending a trial for witchcraft for at least the fourth time (see page 27). It was time for her husband to act. His wife had become a liability, standing between him and the respectable life he desired – a life he probably wanted to share with his housekeeper! The housekeeper, separated from her own husband and probably John Mennin's mistress, sent a servant girl to visit Anne in gaol and give her some oatmeal. Given the poor conditions in prison – food was not provided unless you paid dearly for it or well-wishers brought it – Anne must have been grateful for the meal. Her husband had sent her roast meat and ale for New Year's day, but only two meals in the weeks that followed.

But this final gift contained arsenic. Anne must have sensed that something was wrong, for just before she started to vomit, she said, 'I pray God there is nothing but what is good in the meal'. A woman named Emma or Amy Gaskin watched this and reported it in the morning when Anne was

found dead. Suspicions raised, two Newcastle barber surgeons were brought in. They opened Anne's stomach, and confirmed that the cause of death was arsenic. Meanwhile the gaoler's wife had sifted through the remains of the meal, and also found traces of arsenic. This must have been one of the earliest uses of forensic science in the North-East.

More trouble at the Sherburns'

Thomas Sherburn the watchmaker had another brush with witchcraft. On the very same day the Cudworth children had their fits in the Sherburn house, Emma Gaskin, the woman who watched Anne Mennin die in her prison cell, was found not guilty of bringing about the sickness of the Sherburns' household servant Elizabeth Gibson. All that we know about Emma Gaskin is that she was the wife of a Newcastle skipper. The Sherburns must have been obsessed by witchcraft to the point of paranoia, to turn their attention so swiftly from a lost cause to a new one. Perhaps they believed that the two events were connected. The fact that Emma was in prison again a few months later when Anne died indicates either that someone, whether the Sherburns or another accuser, wanted her out of the way. It is not surprising that Emma and Anne banded together.

In any event, Elizabeth Gibson was still servant to the Sherburns in 1667, when she saw Emma Gaskin, now veteran of at least two spells in prison, again. Emma 'asked something for God's sake', but Elizabeth refused, saying 'she had got too much ill by her already' – presumably referring to the earlier sickness which she believed Emma had caused. Mrs Sherburn looked out from the window and told Emma to leave. Emma then said to the maid, 'she hoped she would either break her neck or hang herself', and very soon afterwards Elizabeth fell ill once more, losing the power of speech and falling into fits in which she saw Emma. Once again, a fascinated audience

The south front of Newgate Prison from a drawing made by T.M. Richardson in 1823. By then the prison, situated approximately where Newgate Street meets Blackett Street, was falling down. The Newcastle witches would have been imprisoned here, while those from Northumberland were probably kept in Hexham or Morpeth, and then moved briefly to the Castle Keep for the assizes.

gathered. On one occasion 'there begun a thing to cry like a hen among the people's feet', and Elizabeth smiled and laughed as the thing made a noise and fluttered against the floor. This time, we sadly do not have the court verdict.

Crossing a witch

At around the same time, Dorothy Heron, the wife of a Newcastle baker and brewer, also suffered for saying the wrong thing to a witch. As her husband Anthony told the tale, widow Jane Simpson came to their house on High Friar Street selling cherries. Dorothy bought a pound of cherries, which cost her eightpence, but she told Jane she knew that she sold the same cherries to other customers for only sevenpence per pound. Jane responded angrily, and went on her way. A few days later, Dorothy became ill, and doctors were unable to diagnose her condition, which seems to have been a peculiar mental complaint. After twenty days she was confined to her bed, 'being sometimes in her sickness raging mad, other times in a laughing and singing condition, other times in a despairing and disconsolate condition and at other times in a very solitary and mute condition'. One morning at 3am she cried out that Jane Simpson and Isabel Atcheson, a labourer's wife, 'were about the bed to carry her away', and her husband had difficulty holding her on the bed. At this point Anthony began to think he could see Isabel Atcheson, recognising her usual green waistcoat. He called upon the Lord, and she disappeared.

Later that day, Dorothy asked to see Jane and Isabel, so Anthony sent for them. He asked Isabel what she had been doing in his house that morning, and she replied that 'it was not her but the devil that was there'. The two women allowed Dorothy to draw blood from them. This had the desired effect as Dorothy was soon able to get up and made a full recovery. Unfortunately, it also proved the guilt of Jane and Isabel. They were both placed in the town gaol, but were released a few weeks later.

Family feuds

Witchcraft is not really a crime that you would expect to be kept within the family. But when family members or branches disagreed, suspicions could follow …

In October 1663, Jane Milburn married a Newcastle baker and brewer – perhaps even a friend of Anthony Heron? Unfortunately it seems that she had not invited her aunt, Dorothy Sharpe or Stranger, to her wedding supper, and this had caused much offence. When Dorothy met one of Jane's servants in town, she sent a message that she would make Jane repent her rudeness. Soon afterwards Jane became ill. Dorothy, she said, bit her and pulled at her bed clothes. A 'thing in the likeness of a grey cat' leaped at her face, but it left when Jane said, 'I defy thee, the devil, and all his works'. Dorothy also appeared in the cellar of Jane's house, and tried to place a rope around her neck, saying 'thy life I seek, thy life I will have'. Jane defied her again, but this time Dorothy replied 'although thou be strong in faith, I'll overcome it at last', before she disappeared. The cat continued to trouble Jane, on several occasions leaping at her, biting her, and even pinning her to the ground for a quarter of

Sandhill around 1870. Some of these houses are 17th century and perhaps Dorothy lived in one of them.

an hour. It was either a very heavy creature, or had supernatural aid!

In November, Jane drew blood from Dorothy. She also formally accused Dorothy before a magistrate. Jane thought, for a time, that the blood letting had cured her. But then in December, the grey cat jumped through a first floor window to where Jane sat working. It then transformed into Dorothy, in 'an old black hat … a green waistcoat and a brownish coloured petticoat'. She said, 'thief, thou got blood of me but I will have blood of thee before I go', and flew at her niece, scratching at her hands. Oddly, she also took Jane's black handkerchief with her when she left.

A month later Dorothy appeared to Jane in her locked bedroom, and asked her for forgiveness, confessing that she had done wrong. She said to Jane, 'if you never trouble me for what I have formerly done to thee I do promise never to molest or trouble thee'. Perhaps the court case was still progressing, and Dorothy was in danger.

This was not the first crisis within the family, as Dorothy hinted when she said she had already 'gotten the life of one in the house' to Jane. Jane had had a cousin, also called Jane, who also married a Milburn. In 1657 Dorothy told this second Jane Milburn that 'she would never see the Sandhill again'. Dorothy lived near the Sandhill, probably on the Close. After this encounter, Jane was ill for six months and finally died blaming Dorothy. When Elizabeth Stranger – this second Jane's mother, and Dorothy's sister-in-law – gave testimony against Dorothy, Dorothy's husband Daniel (Elizabeth's brother-in-law) attacked and abused her. Dorothy was acquitted, both this time and six years later.

Interestingly, Daniel had put up a legal surety for a suspect witch during the

Newcastle witch trials of 1650 (see page 36). He would have been known and remembered in the community as someone who defied the witch hunt, even a possible witch sympathiser. Was it simply coincidence that his own wife was later accused of witchcraft?

MOTHER-IN-LAW TROUBLE

Another old lady whose family drove her, apparently, to witchcraft, was Margaret Milbourne of Morpeth. She lived with her son William who was married to another Margaret. But the two Margarets did not get on, clashing on grounds that sound familiar even today.

One evening the younger woman had gone to wash clothes by the riverbank, and left her mother-in-law holding the baby. The elder woman was unhappy, saying that she was too old to handle the child, and went down to the river to complain that Margaret 'might be better employed to work her own work at home'. The younger woman protested that she would work at home when she could not earn money by working elsewhere. A friend of the younger Margaret,

Dorothy Himers, chipped in her own thought, that there was a 'tough sinew' in the old woman's body – in other words, that she was really quite fit enough to handle the baby. The old woman replied that Dorothy 'would never be old with as much honesty', and left the river bank. On the way she saw her son's servant, Isabel Fletcher, who initially did not recognise her, seeing, she said, 'a white thing coming through the water like a woman'. Margaret asked Isabel to go and see the dame – presumably her mistress, the younger Margaret, or some other relative – to arrange alternative childcare. Isabel refused to do so 'at that time of night'. Margaret replied that if Isabel would not, 'it should be the worse for her'.

This was undoubtedly a miserable family situation, but there was nothing in it to justify an accusation of witchcraft. Then something unfortunate happened. Very soon afterwards, Isabel fell into a swoon, and then a fit; she did this again when she saw Margaret the next day. Also, Dorothy Himers began to fall ill and became unable to work, and she named the elder Margaret as her tormentor, 'pulling her heart with something like a thread'.

THE HOLY OINTMENT

In late 1660, four women were charged with bewitching the one-year old son, and possibly also the wife, of Newcastle labourer Robert Philip. They were Mary Johnson, wife of a Sandgate labourer, Margaret Catherwood and Jane Bambarow – both widowed – and Anne Mennin (whose nasty end has already been described). At this time they were all found innocent, though Anne, at least, spent time in the gaol that would be her last lodging.

In December 1660, Robert Philip fell ill, with chest pains and a headache. We don't know if he already suspected witchcraft, but he was given an ointment for his forehead which must have come from a charmer as it had a holy

A PHYSICIAN FIGHTS A WITCH

Mr Robert Johnson of Newcastle was a rich man, living in a large house on Westgate Street, near St John's church. In 1661, he was suffering from pains in his legs and arms, and had tried several treatments to no effect. He called in physician Nicholas Johnson – probably a relative – who looked at his urine and said he could help. Robert explained that he suspected some foul play. Nicholas agreed, and laid the blame on widow Bely (short for Isabel) Story, whom they had known for many years. Nicholas seems to have asked to be discharged from his medical tasks so that he could instead do something to Isabel which would help Robert recover – perhaps taking blood from her forehead? Robert also decided to prosecute, and just before he did, Isabel said that 'she would give him seven pounds, nay [even] her house she had in Morpeth, if he would not testify'. Isabel, of course, denied any such witchcraft or conversation, and the jury agreed with her.

element. That night, although his doors were closed, three women appeared by his bed – Mary Johnson, Margaret Cotherwood, and one other, unnamed – presumably either Jane or Anne. Margaret told Robert to remove the ointment, 'for it burns me to death'. She 'puffed and blew and cried oh! burnt to the heart'. People believed that a witch gained power by putting something of herself into the spell. This made it strong, but also gave the victim a method of harming the witch, for instance by using a counter charm or religious symbol. Robert told Margaret that if she believed in Jesus Christ, she had nothing to fear from the ointment, but she continued to scream. Mary, less distressed, threatened revenge, but Robert said that 'he trusted in Christ, he was his rock'. Then a disembodied voice said 'whosoever trusted in that rock Jesus Christ shall never perish', and the women vanished. Claiming such direct intervention from God was very unusual, even amongst the highly religious people of the 17th century. But the apparent intervention of the Lord was still not enough to secure a guilty verdict, as Anne survived to bewitch again.

A view of Newcastle in the early 18th century, engraved for the 'Complete English Traveller'.

MOST STRANGELY AND WONDERFULLY HANDLED

In August 1664, in Newcastle, seventeen year old Alice Thompson became 'most strangely and wonderfully handled' – as if some invisible person was moving her limbs – and began to call out that she could see widow Katherine Currey or Potts standing beside her, describing her green clothes. She said that Katherine pulled at her heart, and wanted to carry her away. Alice was losing power of her limbs, and could not eat. At the same time, Alice's mother Eleanor started to see

Katherine around the house as well. When she thought back, she remembered an incident from a few months previously, and suspected that this was another instance of Katherine's witchcraft. They had met in the marketplace, and Katherine had placed her hand on Eleanor's shoulder, saying 'my peck of meal set thy kill on fire'. The kill – presumably a sort of oven – burnt down two days later. It is interesting that she only thought to interpret this as witchcraft months later when other circumstances seemed strange.

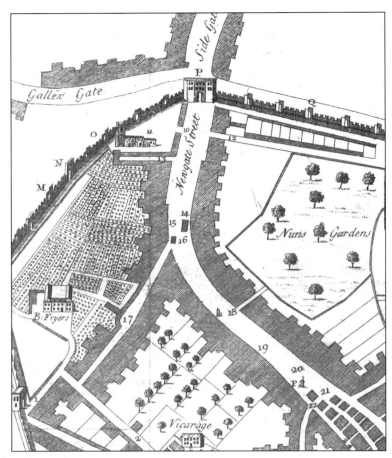

From Henry Bourne's 'History of Newcastle', 1736. 20 indicates the Bigg Market where meal was sold; P indicates the Newgate Prison with Gallow Gate to the left; 11 shows St Andrew's church, the town wall behind it.

Alice's father also reported that he too had seen Katherine, that she had come to the door and said 'that if … Eleanor were not ill enough, she would tear her worse'. Perhaps he stumbled over his words or the scribe got it wrong and they meant the daughter, not the wife. Either way, no verdict survives.

DANCING WITH THE DEVIL

Longwitton man Nicholas Rames must have done something to offend reputed witch Elizabeth Fenwick in 1680, as she told him that she would make him repent. He did not report what he'd done to provoke her threat. Soon his wife Anne fell ill, and said that Elizabeth tormented her, and that she 'rides on her and endeavours to put her onto the floors'. More unusually, she said that she could see Elizabeth dance around the room, with 'a black man, thinking the devil'. Here she meant a man with dark hair, and probably in black clothing, and this was a common image of the devil at that time. Anne said that she must draw Elizabeth's blood, and Elizabeth said 'if blood would do her any good, she might have had it long

since'. She offered a finger, but Anne said 'I will have it upon the brow, where other people get it upon witches'. Anne was weak though, and Nicholas had to help. He had to pierce Anne's brow several times before she bled. Elizabeth asked Nicholas to keep this difficulty to himself (as some might see it as a proof of being a witch). He said he would not bother her again 'if no further prejudice was to him or his wife'. He broke this promise, making a legal accusation, but must have had a change of heart as the case was dropped before it reached court.

THE CROOKED PIN

In 1670, Mary Earnley of Alne (possibly near Alnwick) fell ill. In her pain, she claimed that widow Anne Wilkinson was pricking her with pins. She described seeing Anne, sitting on a chair by the fire, and when others went to visit Anne, they found her exactly as described. Bearing in mind that Anne's home probably had only one room and one chair, this doesn't seem too surprising! Mary also claimed that Anne had killed her sisters, both of whom had died in the previous few months. One of the sisters, it was believed, had been found dead with a black ribbon with a crooked pin on it in her mouth – an obvious bewitching charm.

As so often seems to be the case, Anne already had a reputation. Margaret Wilson said that a few years earlier there had been a great wind. Soon afterwards, she met Anne Wilkinson, who accused Margaret of having asked a wise man to raise the wind against her, and cursed her. The next day, Margaret's milk would not become butter; she herself fell ill and remained so for two years, and her husband died a lingering death.

DEMON WORSHIP AND DEMON ANTICS

HUMAN HORSES

In early 1673, Anne Armstrong, a servant girl from Birksnook or Birchen Nook in the Tyne valley, went to the magistrates with a most extraordinary tale of covens and devil-worship. Her testimony, several thousand words long, was given over several months, each account giving additional details. Some disbelieved her words, but others encouraged her to tell more, being fascinated by her detailed descriptions. Many officials could see the value of having a spy in the camp of the witches. In five months, thirty-one people, both men and women, were accused of witchcraft, most from the Corbridge area.

It all started, Anne said, at Stocksfield market where she had gone to buy eggs. Here a woman 'look'd' her head. Perhaps this means that she gave her a strange look, or perhaps she tried to read Anne's character by phrenology, that is, by the study of the shape of the skull – we don't know.

A few days later, she was moving cows from one field to another when she met a man dressed in ragged clothes. He told her that the woman she had met at Stocksfield was a member of a local coven of witches who wanted her to join them. Their delight was in 'riding in the house in empty wood dishes that had never been wet, and also in eggshells'. They could also 'obtain whatever they desired by swinging on a rope'. He said that they would 'make a horse of her spirit'. He also told her that they could do her no real harm if she did not eat any of their meat – this

Corbridge from the south around 1834. In 1673 31 people from the Corbridge area were accused of witchcraft.

detail bears striking similarity to a lot of fairy tales and folk beliefs. She would not be able to tell anyone about this, until one day, 'when she laid down in a field with her apron coat over her head', she found a piece of cheese by her side and ate it.

From that day on, Anne was prone to fits of unconsciousness. It was a few months before the coven turned their attention to her, and forced her to go to the first of a series of meetings at various locations, most often Riding Mill. A member of the coven would come to her at night, usually in human shape but once as a grey cat who knocked her down. The witch would place a bridle on her, which forced her into the shape of a horse, and then rode upon her cross-legged to meet with the others (this kind of experience is where the expression 'hag-ridden' comes from). At these gatherings, thirteen women would come, each one riding a 'horse'. They were then joined by a 'long black man' who they called their protector, who sat on a golden chair. Once the meeting was larger, a gathering of several covens, each with its own 'devil' at the head. So rather than being attended by the devil himself, Satan had obviously delegated the job to his workforce.

One day, Anne found the piece of cheese as the ragged man had said, and went to the magistrates. This did not actually help her, as the visitations continued, but it does mean we have a very detailed account of what she said happened at the coven's meetings.

Firstly, the witches danced, sometimes in their own shape, and sometimes becoming animals, like hares, cats or mice. Anne was made to sing to accompany this strange sight. She was also offered a 'lease' of sixty years of life, in which she would not want for money, and also a cow which would give the milk of ten, if she joined them. It must have been quite a temptation for a servant girl, but the witches clearly misjudged her feelings on the matter!

A favourite activity, as the old man had suggested, was to swing on a rope hanging from the roof, wishing for a particular type of food and drink, which instantly appeared. Each person seems to have had three goes at this. They could choose anything they desired, except for water. Many of the women asked for their favourite food, foods which were luxury items to the peasants of rural Northumberland – Lucy Thompson wanted boiled capon, Anne Foster cheese, Ann Dryden currants and sack (sweet wine), and so on.

Mainly though, they wanted to please the devil who sat

The deposition or 'information' of Anne Armstrong, written down from her actual words as she was questioned.

with them. They recited the Lord's Prayer backwards for him. The main activity of the night was in telling the devil what evil deeds they had committed for him, in exchange for the lease of years they received. The devil praised some, and punished any who had not performed enough acts of wickedness. Anne gave a long list of different witches and their activities. Some had gained control of animals, making them sicken and die, sometimes by flying around the animal in the form of a swallow. Others had damaged property, or made individuals fall ill or die.

The authorities were divided about Anne's testimony. Some seemed rather suspicious, and made her re-swear the truth, especially as all the 'witches' they questioned gave flat denials. Others encouraged her to testify and implicate more people. They brought before her other suspected witches, asking her if she had seen them at witches' meetings. One witch who was brought before her breathed on her and Anne fell into a swoon.

Anne also found allies, whether genuine victims and believers, or just people who wanted to harm the witch's reputation. She sent messages to individuals whom she had

heard had been bewitched or lost animals, and correctly identified their troubles. Some were willing to testify that a swallow had flown around their beasts before they sickened.

Anne's story is most unusual, as many elements of it were rarely heard of in England. Scotland and France had trials involving tales of sabbats, covens and devil worship, but in England it seems that most people did not associate these things with witches. Instead they thought of lone cursing women appearing at the bedsides of the sick. It is interesting to wonder where Anne got her ideas from – some parts were similar to the Scots tradition, but given a unique local slant, with country dancing and good broth replacing orgiastic feasting.

Anne's story was so wild, so vivid, that most of the justices were not convinced. She was just an illiterate serving girl, probably only in her teens, and we have to wonder whether she was just seeking attention – she was certainly treated as special, during her moment of fame – or simply delusional. It seems that no convictions ever came from her testimony, although one 'witch' died in gaol.

THE DEVIL AND HIS TORMENTS

Satan could work his will without the help of human agents. One example occurred in 1641, just over the border into Cumberland at Edenbyres near Derwentwater, according to the pamphlet 'Newes out of the Bishopric of Durham, or Strange Miracles'. It is a moral tale of the power of God in defeating the wiles of the devil, but spectacular enough to make the story worthy of Hollywood.

Stephen Hooper was too ill to manage all of his property properly, so he sent his wife Margaret out to a farm at Hanstonueth. When she returned she had some ideas about how things could be improved. Finding her husband in moderate health, she began to talk, about the farm, about an old coin her son had found the previous week, and other things. Somehow she didn't stop talking. Her talk became more and more wild and she continued for some days. Stephen began to worry about her health, and persuaded her to pray with him. But Margaret grew more agitated and eventually she seemed to be entering a fit, writhing on the bed and foaming at the mouth, making the whole chamber shake. Stephen had to call for her sister and others to help him. Half an hour later she came to, with tales of having been followed by a bear with no head. Her husband and friends persuaded her to say the Lord's Prayer, and then try to rest. The fits continued, on and off, for the next few days.

On Sunday, just as the night-time candle burned out, Margaret cried out that she saw something like a snail, 'carrying fire in a most wonderful sort'. Stephen called other family members into the room, to help to comfort his wife, and watch in case of further outbursts. Margaret kept asking her family if they could see the devil, and assured them they would 'see something by and by', no matter how much they talked about the power of God. Then they heard a noise like 'the coming of four or five carts' in the street below; and

Strangely, a headless bear was not an unprecedented 'vision' to have. This illustration comes from a pamphlet of 1614.

Stephen saw something by the bed, 'much like a bear, but it had no head or tail, half a yard in height and half a yard in length'. It is difficult to imagine quite what this creature looked like. Stephen picked up a stool, and struck at it. The blow sounded 'as if he had struck a featherbed'. Then it reached Margaret, took hold of her, and 'rolled her to and fro in the chamber, and under the bed'. It ended the display by placing her head between her legs, and rolling her through the room 'like a hoop', and down the stairs into another room. It's a pity that Stephen wasn't brave enough to follow and try to rescue his wife. Instead, he and the other witnesses stayed at the head of the stairs too terrified to follow, for quarter of an hour. There was 'a horrible stink', and flames in the hallway,

so they covered their mouths and waited, until Margaret called up to Stephen that the beast had gone. Stephen, still too scared to go downstairs, called back, 'in the name of God, come up to me', and she returned. They put her in bed, four of them holding the bedclothes down, and waited.

But the candle flickered dimly, and suddenly the window opened, and Margaret was out of bed, her legs wrapped around the central pillar of the window and hanging out of the house. The watchers heard a sound like a knock on a tub, and saw a 'great fire' around the floor, smelling foul.

At last Stephen and his brother found a little courage, and commanded the devil to leave in the name of the Father, Son and Holy Ghost. They called on God to help them. They managed to pull Margaret back into the room. She looked out of the window again, saying, 'methink I see a little child', and when the others looked out they too saw a child, 'with a very bright shining countenance, casting a great light into the chamber'. They fell to the ground and thanked God for his assistance. Margaret went back to bed, where she asked for forgiveness, saying that it was because of her sins that the devil could torment her. She was not troubled again.

THE WITCHFINDER

The 1640s were a time of great uncertainty. As the civil war raged on, authority seemed to be in danger of falling apart, and people became anxious about their security. One way this showed itself was as an increased worry about witchcraft – and there were those willing to exploit that for money. This is what happened in 1649 when Newcastle was host to one of the biggest witch trials England ever saw. The story starts, however, in Berwick.

In July 1649, Berwick town council sent for a Scottish witch finder – whose name we sadly never find out – to find the town's witches (some argue that he was a man named

John Kincaid, who does appear in Scottish records at around the same date, but there is no proof of this). He was still there in September, when the local MP sent a letter on the subject. He said the man 'professeth himself an artist in that way' (in finding witches), and was given 20 shillings per 'witch' he found. In Berwick he identified and examined thirty women, a few of whom confessed that they were witches 'but with no harm to anybody'. These were probably women who used simple charms combining prayers, traditional rhymes, and herbal remedies. Two or three more said 'they were at Preston Battle, made many a Scot fell that day'. At Preston, the king had suffered a great defeat, and his allies put it about that witchcraft had been used against him. Confessing or not, all went to gaol pending trial, but records were lost during the civil war, so no more is known.

But the witchfinder's career continued. During that summer, the Puritan corporation of Newcastle requested his services. He arrived by December, again promised twenty shillings for each witch he identified. Ralph Gardner, a Newcastle man with a grudge against the corporation, published testimonies describing what happened next.

When the Scotsman arrived, the magistrate's bell-man went through town announcing that anyone with a complaint against a witch should bring her to the town hall. Thirty accused women were assembled and stripped. The witchfinder stuck pins in them to see if they bled. Witches were thought to have a 'mark', an unusual bloodless spot where their familiar suckled, so a lack of blood and feeling was taken as proof of guilt. In practice, a lot of old ladies must have had some sort of skin blemish which would serve the witchfinder's purpose. If not, there was always the possibility of using a retractable pin with a point which would not penetrate the skin. Twenty-seven of the women were found guilty, and taken away to await trial. Two were considered

The Guildhall, which was also the town hall, on Newcastle's Sandhill as it looked between 1658 and 1796. The 'witches' would have been brought to the Guildhall to be examined in 1649, though not to this building.

The medieval Guildhall was demolished in 1655 after being damaged in the Civil War. Anne Mennin and the later witches were probably brought to the building above.

innocent, and the last became something of a problem. The lieutenant colonel overseeing the process – who was both a strong Baptist, and an ex-military surgeon – happened to notice this 'personable and good-like woman', and protested that surely she was not a witch (since the Scotsman had said that he could tell a witch by her looks). The witchfinder said 'she was, for the town said she was, and therefore he would try her'. He pulled her skirts over her head, leaving her half-naked, and put a pin in her thigh, which did not bleed or attract her notice. The lieutenant felt that this was because the blood had all rushed away because of the shame of being exposed in front of so many people and the fear of being called a witch. He insisted that the test be done again, in a more decent manner, and this time the woman bled, and was cleared.

The witchfinder also went into Durham, and almost forty individuals were formally accused in the two towns. Eighteen – seventeen women and one man – were hanged on the town moor in August 1650. At least two more 'witches' were executed in Durham in 1651 which may be connected with the witchfinder's activities. One more must have been buried in Gateshead, where the parish register records a payment of sixpence 'for a grave for a witch'. This is a high price for a pauper burial – perhaps special precautions were made to make sure that she did not rise again to cause trouble, just as were taken with the bodies of suicides at this time.

The tide was turning, however. Even in Newcastle there were those opposed to the witchfinder's actions, like Elinor Loumsdale, who was prosecuted for trying to dissuade a witness from giving evidence against a witch, and who later told her story to Gardner to help him write his book. And elsewhere, things would get tougher. The witchfinder went next to try women in rural Northumberland, but Justice of the Peace, Henry Ogle, tried to arrest him, and he escaped back to

St Andrew's church in 1723. Exactly where the unfortunate 'witches' were buried is unknown.

Scotland. Gardner says that here he was hanged, after confessing to causing the death of 220 English and Scots women.

We have details of the accusations made in only one case. This concerns Jane Martin, who was one of those hanged on town moor and buried in St Andrews' churchyard, Newcastle. Her story is a small part of a pamphlet written to expound the sins of a small group of 'witches' who were caught up in the

This illustration is taken from Ralph Gardner's 'England's Grievance Discovered in Relation to the Coal Trade' of 1655. He was keen to condemn Newcastle Corporation and the witch-hunting episode provided him with much ammunition. Apart from Newcastle, only Pendle in Lancashire and East Anglia witnessed such intense pursuit of witches.

The key to the picture explains that A represents the hangman, B is the bellman, C are the two sergeants and D is the witch-finder taking money for his work.

panic of 1650. This pamphlet recounts a different version of events also told in a confession. While torture was not allowed under English law, the woman, perhaps old and confused, may have been kept walking about without sleep for many hours, as happened under the East Anglian witchfinder Matthew Hopkins at around the same date. She was probably at least promised a lighter sentence or heavenly forgiveness if she confessed. The story below combines the confession and the pamphlet.

Margaret White lived in Chatton, in north Northumberland. She told the town clerk of Berwick that in 1645, the devil had come to her in the shape of a man dressed in blue, who took her hand and said that she should never want for anything. He gave her a familiar, a black greyhound, and sometimes slept with her. They also held parties, in which they, along with Margaret's sister, Jane Martin, and Dorothy Swinhoe, would eat, drink and make merry, and plot the bewitching and killing of children and adults.

The success of their spells is described by Mrs Moore in her account, 'Wonderful News from the North' (wonderful here means strange, not good). The author was probably the mother of the Muschamp children, the children who suffered most, although the family situation was complex. The fact that the pamphlet was written by a woman makes it extremely unusual.

At Michaelmas 1645, Margaret Muschamp began to fall regularly into trances in which she saw angels. The girl also lost the use of her limbs sometimes, and even though she did not eat, she did not lose weight. That Christmas, her brother George became seriously ill, while Margaret found herself in visions battling with dragon, horse, bear or cow. During one trance, she wrote down Jo. Hu. and Do. Swo., and said that her life depended upon having two drops of the blood of one of these people.

The family interpreted these names as meaning that the known witch Dorothy Swinhoe was responsible, and that John Hutton of (North) Sunderland, a man who, 'it was suspected, could do more than God allowed of', should be consulted. The family went to John, who agreed that Dorothy was to blame, saying that she had also killed Lady Margery Hambleton, Mrs Muschamp's sister, because Dorothy had believed that her own son would gain property through this action (this raises the possibility that the two families were related). John allowed Margaret to prick him, though she had to take the two drops from his arm because no blood appeared when she nicked his forehead. He even went with the Muschamps to Spittal to let George – who was too ill to be moved – draw his blood.

The family then took the story to Justice Forster. Oddly, his next actions appear to have been to arrest and examine John Hutton, and to show the examination to Dorothy Swinhoe, rather than arrest her too. Soon afterwards, the unfortunate Hutton died in prison. Hutton had never been accused of anything, in fact he'd only tried to help, so this seems particularly unfair. Margaret Muschamp predicted his death in one of her continuing visions. She also began to give complex religious discourses.

Mrs Moore was determined that Dorothy should not get away, and had her arrested again in Berwick, but she talked herself free. The bewitched Margaret, seeing this, had yet another fit, and cried out that her torment would be eased if Dorothy were brought to justice. The judge was not convinced. He thought that Margaret was faking. Mrs Moore said that it was the scepticism of those surrounding her that led her to write the pamphlet – even her husband was not convinced, and she felt that the witch Dorothy had hardened his heart.

Margaret's symptoms soon became even more dramatic and terrifying. She vomited 'stones, coals, bricks, lead, straw, quills full of pins, tow and virginal wire, all full of pins'. A virginal is an ancestor of the piano, and tow is flax or hemp, rough fibres often made into rope. Vomiting of strange objects in this way was thought to be a sign of demonic possession or harmful bewitching. It would certainly have given her a very sore throat!

The children, Margaret and George, both recovered in early 1647, without any explanation. This was not the end, however. In 1648, Mrs Moore accused Dorothy Swinhoe of bewitching to death the infant Sybil Moore. This seems to be

An extract from Speed's map of Northumberland of 1610 showing the area described by Margaret Moore in her pamphlet 'Wonderful News from the North'.

the child that Margaret White referred to in her confession, when she said 'they could not get their desires perfected, and they could not take the child of one Mrs Moore within the womb', having to wait until it was born.

It was soon after this that Margaret White confessed. Dorothy was taken to gaol, but we don't know what happened to her next. As the justices seemed doubtful of Mrs Moore's claims, perhaps she was lucky. Her sister, Jane Martin, certainly was not. She seems to have been accused at the quarter sessions court of Alnwick, probably while the witchfinder was there on his journey between Berwick and Newcastle, found guilty and taken to Newcastle to be hanged.

It is said that another witchfinder – John Stearne, the assistant of the notorious Witchfinder General, Matthew Hopkins – came to the area in 1652. However, despite his remarkable deeds in East Anglia, he does not seem to have caused as much fuss in Northumberland as his Scottish contemporary, and the whole tale may be a later invention.

SLANDER AND DEFAMATION

Not all accusations of witchcraft were instantly believed by those around. So making an accusation might just lead to your own prosecution for slander, then called defamation. In 1687, several people stated that John Richardson of Ellington publicly called widow Jane Blackburn a witch, and said 'he wished he could get blood of her'. His wife agreed. They were tried for defamation.

And in 1709, Robert Johnson of Blackhall was convinced that his ailing cows were bewitched, and went around saying so. This report was so widely believed that the alleged witch, Christopher Middleton of Lee, who hired himself out as a farm labourer, was finding it hard to find work. When Christopher's wife Elinor chanced upon Robert, she asked him why he was accusing her husband, but he simply repeated the claim, and said 'I will prove it'. His daughter-in-law chimed in her agreement. Christopher took the defamation before a

HOW TO KEEP YOUR COWS SAFE

Cows, being valuable possessions prone to mysterious illness, were a favourite target of witches – in 1668 Alice Armstrong of Shotton, County Durham, was tried for bewitching an ox to death. But measures could be taken.

Elizabeth Douglas of Brampton, a wise woman of 1800, recommended slitting a bewitched cow's tail and putting rowan wood in the wound. An easier option might be to prevent bewitching by putting salt on the cow's back. Also, you could remove a spell which prevented a cow from giving milk by milking it over a south-running stream.

LATER MAGIC

magistrate.

Scepticism grew, especially amongst the educated, that the devil could or did work his will via old women. The last person hanged for witchcraft in England died in 1685, and the last trial was in 1712. The witchcraft laws were repealed in 1736. But this did not stop plenty of people from believing in harmful magic. The parish register of Holy Island records that in July 1691 William Cleugh was bewitched to death, although no-one was ever tried.

People could still be punished harshly for fraud, or 'false pretences', if they claimed magic abilities – they were pilloried four times in a market square. The pillory trapped the criminal

in a standing position, hands and head locked into place, for public ridicule and significant discomfort. Four women were pilloried in late 18th century Newcastle for false pretences and telling fortunes. One of them, Susanna Fleming, was over eighty years old when she was placed in the pillory for fortune telling in 1758. Either because of her constricting clothes, or because she was half fainting, she nearly strangled, and had to be rescued from the pillory by a passing sailor. These events were recounted in the local newspaper, the *Newcastle Journal*. Susanna petitioned for a reprieve from the rest of her sentence, citing the state of her health and saying it may well be her death to be pilloried again. Her petition was also signed by other reputable locals. Most such 'criminals' were women, but in 1755, James Lawson was made to stand in the pillory four times, for 'pretending to tell fortunes and find lost goods'.

The Reverend John Brand was very interested in the customs of his flock, and wrote a book, *Observations on Popular Antiquities*, which mentions witches. In the 1780s, Brand was visiting the ruins of Brinkburn abbey when he met 'a reputed witch in a lonely cottage by the side of the wood, where the parish had placed her to save expenses and keep her out of the way'. He made enquiries in the village of Brinkburn, and with some persistence he found out that 'everyone was afraid of her cat, and that she herself was thought to have an evil eye, and that it was dangerous to meet her on a morning "black fasting"'. Black fasting was a ritual fast which was intended to secure a death. Most references to it come from

Brinkburn Priory around 1750.

the early 16th century, and in 1577 the Bishop of Durham specifically forbade it, but obviously belief in it lasted a lot longer.

Not all witches were social outcasts, and even the threat of punishment did not stop cunning folk from going about their business. We don't really know how many people continued to practise magic, but a little down the coast, in Whitby, there were eight resident wise-women in 1810. There wouldn't have been so many in one place unless a lot of people still believed in the power of their charms and would pay for magical help.

In Newcastle the most famous cunning man of the 19th century was Black Jacky Johnson, who claimed to have charms for everything from fortune telling and wart charming to invisibility and finding stolen goods (for more on Black Jacky, see *Nightmare on Grey Street*, details on page 2). He did, however, face a lot of competition.

One high-profile charmer of the 19th century was Nannie Scott, who lived in 'hovel' on the coast near Sunderland, in the 1830s. She offered a wide range of services, from love-charms and curses to astrological advice and a remedy based on treacle. Living so near a fishing town, her attempts to provide fair winds were much in demand. She kept a black dog, and a cat. She worked with 'an air of solemn strong-mindedness that bore down any approach to discredit.'

A dapper local rival to Nannie Scott was John Wrightson who practised in the 1830s and 1840s. He had a farm at Stokesley, just over the border into North Yorkshire, but he drew clients from right across Yorkshire and County Durham. He was trained as a vet, but also cured people and cattle, found lost goods, removed spells, and comforted the anxious.

Here is an example of his methods, used to cure a man thought bewitched. It is not a good story for the squeamish.

'Clippings from every finger and toe nail of the patient, with hair from each temple, and the crown of his head, were stuffed into the throat of a pigeon which had previously been placed between the patient's feet, and there had died at once, thus attesting the witchery from which he was suffering. The bird's bill was rivetted with three pins, and then the wise man thrust a pin into its breast, to reach the heart, everybody else in the room in turn following his example. An opening was then made in the fire, and the pigeon dropped into it. The wise man began to read aloud Psalms from the Prayer Book, and a loud scratching began outside.'

This implies that the magic had sent the evil spirit away, and it was now outside – although the patient himself cynically suggested that the noise came from the Wrightson's own dog!

Far from being a scruffy and disreputable outcast,

Wrightson seems to have been well respected. He cultivated a striking impression to help attract clients and get their confidence. In public, he dressed like a dandy, with 'a scarlet coat, a long white waistcoat and full starched shirt frill, crimson knee breeches and white stockings'. But when giving consultations, he pandered to popular expectation. He wore a long robe, and the room was decorated with a human skull, a globe, and bunches of dried herbs. Those around described him as 'a man of not unkindly nature, with a pungent flavour of rough humour about him, shrewd and observant'. He was also known to be a strongly religious man, godfather to many children, and this was not seen as a contradiction. He tried to train up a son to follow in his footsteps, but in the face of his son's lack of interest (or love for pigeons!) he eventually gave his learned texts to a nephew. This lad tried to keep up his uncle's business, but in the end was discredited.

Cruelty to pigeons was also central to the method of 'Black Willie' of Hartlepool. His activities in 1861 are known because they were recorded by a local reverend, who heard the strange story of a parishioner accused by her neighbours of witchcraft.

The woman said that her neighbours had lost two horses to suspicious illness, and so consulted Black Willie. To discover the witch he first blocked up every hole into the house, even keyholes. Then a pigeon was produced, and each member of the family stuck pins into its heart. The next person to pass by the door would be the guilty party. The poor parishioner was next, and so her neighbours began to abuse her as a witch.

Dr Johnson, a Sunderland physician of around 1840 wrote a letter detailing events in his town. He said that a Southwick labourer had a toddler which fell ill with a wasting disease, and the family suspected bewitching. They took the advice of a local charmer, an Irishman. He told them to come to his room with the child at midnight. Within a circle of candles and astrological symbols, he took the naked child in his arms. Here he said charms, annointed him with an ointment on breast and forehead, waved a magic wand, and spoke to a patron spirit to ask aid for the boy.

Most charmers we know about were at the high, intellectual and prosperous end of a spectrum that still reached down to ragged old women who would offer charms for food. The names and lives of such people are rarely recorded. But they still had enemies. In 1770 an Alnwick man admitted that: 'a poor old woman was nearly bled to death by our thrusting a large pin into a vein in her temples, we having long suspected her a witch and the author of several accidents which befell us.'

In 1868, a family from Framwellgate Moor applied to a policeman for permission to draw blood from an old woman who they thought had bewitched their daughter. He refused, so they went to wise man Jonah Stoker for his help. Together they then went to make the witch bleed. In some ways, little had changed in two and a half centuries.

SOME NORTHERN CURES, LOVE-CHARMS – AND A HANDFUL OF WARNINGS

In uncertain times omens or portents of the future are taken seriously. In the same way, charms for warding off ill fortune are as prevalent. Here are just a few local ones from earlier days … but next time you touch wood, or avoid a ladder, remember our ancestors had to look out for many more signs of danger.

In 1770 a writer from Alnwick commented on the amount of superstitions there were:

> 'A hare could not start or a magpie chatter in my walks which I did not interpret as prognosticating some calamity. A couple of straws lying across each other in my path were as terrible as a drawn sword in the hand of a murderous ruffian.'

A cure for a hand hurt on a rusty nail, as suggested by a Winlaton cunning man in the mid-19th century:

Take the nail to a blacksmith to be filed and polished, and to be rubbed before sunrise and after sunset each day. This will cure the wound.

An early 19th century cure for a toothache:

Rub it with a piece of wood taken from Winter's gibbet (William Winter was hanged in 1791; his gibbet still stands at Elsdon now with a wooden head!).

A mid-19th century method to see a future husband:

Eat nothing all day, but instead boil an egg, extract the yolk and fill the cavity with salt. Eat the egg, shell and all (!) and then walk backwards into bed, saying:

> *'Sweet Agnes, work thy fast, if ever ever I be to marry man*
> *Or man be to marry me, I hope him this night to see …'*

Or if eggs are not to your taste, eat a raw red herring, bones and all …

Or go to Wooler, to perform a charm at the local well, with your lover. Here bend a pin and throw it into the well, making a wish for a speedy or happy marriage. The *Newcastle Daily Journal* in 1893 noted that there were so many bent pins in the bottom of the well, plenty of people must still be following the custom.

And remember these warnings:

Never use your right forefinger to apply anything to a wound, as it is venomous.

On New Year's Day don't take a light out of the house or throw anything out, even ashes or dirty water.

Don't cross knives or there will be a death or a quarrel. If you leave a knife blade upwards you will harm the spirits in the air.

Cross your fingers when you see a white horse. You can uncross them when you see a brown horse or a dog, when you can have a wish.

I DEFY THEE!

As well as believing that witches were neighbours living in the community, people told (and still tell) stories about witches who were long dead. Some aspects of these tales will be familiar from previous stories, others are based on misconceptions, like the idea that witches were burnt. Sometimes these stories had a tiny root in reality.

For instance, Janet Pereson of Wallsend, the woman who washed shirts to banish fairies, may have influenced a later legend about a Wallsend witch. Sir Francis Delaval, who died in 1771, used to tell the tale that an ancestor in times past had gone to see why the Wallsend chapel was lit up, and there discovered a coven of witches. They seemed to be preparing charms by hacking up the corpse of a woman. Delaval burst into the room, and the witches tried to flee. He managed to capture one, and she was condemned to burn on Seaton Sands, a place which some say saw several witch burnings, and worse tortures, over the years.

On the way to the stake, she begged for one last favour – two unused wooden platters. Having heard Anne Armstrong's testimony, we are not surprised at what happened next – she put them under her feet just as the fire was lit, said a spell, and began to rise away. But it happened that one of the platters had been dipped in running water, and so it gave way and the witch was thrown back into the flames.

This is all rather fanciful, an invention of the adventures of an ancestor. But people really might be afraid of witches desecrating churches. How else can we explain the font found buried under rubble at Chevington church, except as a means to ensure that no-one could put it to improper use?

The only other likely explanation is that it was placed in the ground to increase the sanctity and good luck of the church site while it was still in use – not so very different a purpose from that of Alderman Fenwick's mummified cat! Whether using charms to try to increase well being, or whether trying to prevent the actions of those in league with the devil, such legacies underline how important the supernatural world of witches and magic were to our ancestors.

Witchy, witchy, I defy thee!
Four fingers round my thumb,
Let me go quietly by thee!

(anti-witch rhyme from Teesdale, around 1800)

Seaton Sands, a bleak place, in 1894.

SOURCES AND FURTHER READING

All the stories told here were written down very near to the time that events took place – that is why they give us such a clear idea of how people thought. But where were they written?

Almost all of the tales of bewitching come from 'informations'– that is, witness statements – given to the Assizes Court. These records can be found in the Public Record Office, reference ASSI 45. Most of these are reprinted in the Surtees Society volume for 1862, 'Depositions from York Castle', ed. J. Raine. A few cases went to the quarter sessions – these can be found in Northumberland Record Office, Morpeth, reference QSB. A few more come from church court records, also reprinted by the Surtees Society, volumes for 1845, ed. J. Raine, or in P. Hair, *Before the Bawdy Court*.

Other tales come from a wide range of books and pamphlets. These have been named within the text. A couple of these pamphlets are summarised in C. Ewen's *Witchcraft and Demonianism*. This book also tells us the verdicts in most of the Assizes cases.

A huge amount has been written about witches, ranging from books of legends and folk stories, to academic analysis of particular court cases. There are a couple of books which have been especially helpful in the writing of this book, which combine readability and anecdotes with historical accuracy, and they are recommended to anyone wanting to learn more about witches and magic in times past. These are J. Sharpe's *Instruments of Darkness*, a recent overview of the subject of witches, and K. Thomas's *Religion and the Decline of Magic*, a classic work on the whole supernatural world of the English, from superstition to demons and fairies.

Other works which have been helpful include G. Morgan and P. Rushton's *Rogues, Thieves and the Rule of Law* – which looks at crime and punishment in the North-East in the 18th century, R. Hutton's *The Triumph of the the Moon*, which includes a rare discussion of cunning men in the nineteenth century, and P. Rushton's article, 'Crazes and Quarrels', in the Bulletin of the Durham County Local History Society, 1983, which is specifically about North-Eastern witches and especially interesting on the witchfinder of 1650.